bitesize

MACARONS, CAKE POPS
& CUTE THINGS

hardie grant books

MELBOURNE · LONDON

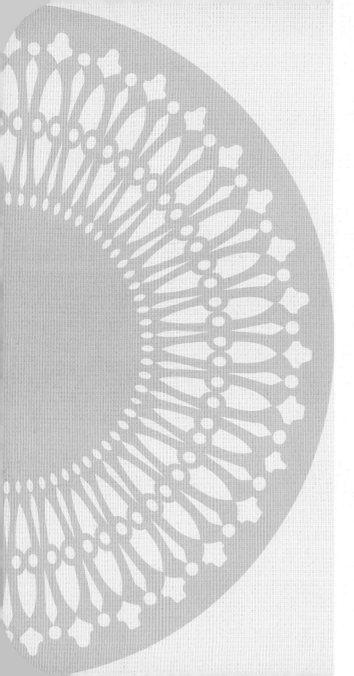

contents

raspberry macarons
with white chocolate

Line 2 baking trays with baking paper. Process the almond meal and icing sugar in a food processor until combined, then sift twice. Place the eggwhite in the bowl of an electric mixer and beat on medium speed until frothy, then increase the speed while gradually adding the caster sugar. Continue beating until stiff peaks form, then mix in the raspberry extract and enough colouring for desired effect. Fold one-third into the almond mixture and combine well. Gently fold through the remaining eggwhite mixture; it should be glossy and thick, not thin and runny.

Transfer to a piping bag fitted with a 5 mm (¼ inch) plain nozzle and pipe 3 cm (1¼ inch) circles about 3 cm (1¼ inches) apart onto the trays. Leave at room temperature for 1–6 hours (depending on the humidity) or until a crust forms; the macarons should no longer be sticky to the touch.

Preheat the oven to 140°C (275°F/Gas 1). Bake the macarons for 15–18 minutes until they rise slightly. Immediately slide the macarons and paper off the trays and onto wire racks to cool completely.

Meanwhile, to make the ganache, place the chocolate and cream in the top of a double boiler over medium heat and stir until melted and smooth. Refrigerate for 25–35 minutes or until firm but pliable. Add the raspberry extract and jam and mix well.

Transfer to a small piping bag fitted with a 1 cm (½ inch) plain nozzle and pipe about 1 teaspoon onto half of the macarons. Sandwich with the remaining macarons.

MAKES ABOUT 30

120 g (4¼ oz) almond meal (ground almonds)

220 g (7¾ oz) icing (confectioners') sugar

110 g (3¾ oz) eggwhite

30 g (1 oz) caster (superfine) sugar

2 teaspoons natural raspberry extract

pink food colouring, paste or powdered is preferable

WHITE CHOCOLATE GANACHE

120 g (4¼ oz) white chocolate, chopped

2½ tablespoons pouring (single) cream

2 teaspoons natural raspberry extract

3 teaspoons raspberry jam

dulce de leche cupcakes

Preheat the oven to 180°C (350°F/Gas 4). Line 42 x 30 ml (1 fl oz/ ⅛ cup) capacity mini-muffin holes with paper cases.

To make the cupcakes, sift the flour, baking powder and cinnamon together into a bowl.

Place the butter and sugar in the bowl of an electric mixer and beat on medium speed for 2–3 minutes or until light and creamy. Add the eggs, one at a time, beating well after each addition. Add the flour mixture, in 2 batches, alternating with the buttermilk, scraping down the sides of the bowl as required. Add the vanilla extract and combine well.

Transfer the batter to a large piping bag fitted with a 1 cm (½ inch) plain nozzle and pipe into the cases, filling them three-quarters full. Bake for 10–12 minutes or until lightly golden and they spring back lightly to the touch. Cool in the tins for 1–2 minutes, then turn out onto wire racks to cool completely.

Fill a piping bag fitted with a small plain nozzle tip with the dulce de leche. Insert the nozzle into each cupcake and pipe a little dulce de leche into the centre.

To make the frosting, place the butter, icing sugar, cream and vanilla extract in the bowl of an electric mixer and beat on medium speed for 3–4 minutes. Increase the speed to high and beat until light and creamy. Reduce the speed, add the dulce de leche and beat to combine. Transfer to a large piping bag fitted with a small star nozzle and pipe onto the cupcakes. Dust with the extra cinnamon.

NOTE: Dulce de leche is available from Latin American grocers and gourmet food shops.

MAKES 42

185 g (6½ oz/1¼ cups) plain (all-purpose) flour

¾ teaspoon baking powder

2½ teaspoons ground cinnamon, plus extra, for dusting

125 g (4½ oz) unsalted butter, at room temperature

185 g (6½ oz/1 cup lightly packed) soft brown sugar

2 eggs

125 ml (4½ fl oz/½ cup) buttermilk

1 teaspoon natural vanilla extract

125 ml (4½ fl oz/½ cup) dulce de leche (see note)

DULCE DE LECHE FROSTING

125 g (4½ oz) unsalted butter, at room temperature

375 g (13 oz/3 cups) icing (confectioners') sugar

3 tablespoons pouring (single) cream

2 teaspoons natural vanilla extract

125 ml (4½ fl oz/½ cup) dulce de leche (see note)

lemon cheesecakes
with blueberry sauce

Preheat the oven to 150°C (300°F/Gas 2). Line 30 x 30 ml (1 fl oz/⅛ cup) capacity mini-muffin holes with paper cases.

Combine the crushed biscuit and butter in a bowl. Divide between the cases and refrigerate for 15 minutes.

Place the cream cheese and sugar in the bowl of an electric mixer and beat on medium–high speed for 2 minutes. Reduce the speed, add the egg and beat well, scraping down the sides of the bowl as required. Add the flour, lemon juice and zest and combine well.

Transfer the mixture to a large piping bag fitted with a 3 cm (1¼ inch) plain nozzle and pipe into the paper cases, filling them three-quarters full. Top each cheesecake with 2–3 blueberries, slightly pushing them into the mixture. Bake for 15 minutes or until set. Cool in the tins for 5 minutes, then turn out onto wire racks and cool for 30 minutes. Refrigerate for at least 3 hours.

Meanwhile, to make the sauce, place all of the ingredients in a saucepan over low heat and stir gently until the sugar has dissolved and the blueberries release some of their juices. Using a slotted spoon, remove the berries and set aside. Increase the heat to high and cook until the liquid has reduced by one-third. Pour over the berries, leave to cool completely, then refrigerate until chilled.

To serve, spoon 1 tablespoon of sauce over each cheesecake.

MAKES 30

90 g (3¼ oz) gingersnap biscuits, crushed

40 g (1½ oz) unsalted butter, melted

250 g (9 oz/1 cup) cream cheese, at room temperature

110 g (3¾ oz/½ cup) caster (superfine) sugar

1 egg

1½ tablespoons plain (all-purpose) flour

1 tablespoon lemon juice

finely grated zest of 1 lemon

150 g (5½ oz/1 cup) fresh blueberries

BLUEBERRY SAUCE

150 g (5½ oz/1 cup) fresh blueberries

55 g (2 oz/¼ cup) caster (superfine) sugar

3 tablespoons lemon juice

1 tablespoon blueberry jam

profiteroles with
chocolate-espresso sauce

To make the profiteroles, preheat the oven to 210°C (415°F/Gas 6–7). Line 2 baking trays with baking paper. Place the butter, sugar and 250 ml (9 fl oz/1 cup) water in a saucepan over medium heat and bring to the boil. Add the flour and stir vigorously with a wooden spoon until the dough comes together to form a ball. Continue stirring for 2–3 minutes, then remove from the heat. Transfer to the bowl of an electric mixer fitted with a paddle attachment. Add the eggs, one at a time, beating well after each addition.

Transfer the warm dough to a large piping bag fitted with a 1 cm (½ inch) plain nozzle and pipe 2.5 cm–3 cm (1 inch–1¼ inch) rounds about 2.5 cm (1 inch) apart onto the trays. Bake for 15 minutes, then reduce the heat to 180°C (350°F/Gas 4) and bake for a further 7–10 minutes. To test if the profiteroles are cooked, cut one in half; it should be hollow and dry inside, not eggy. Cool completely on wire racks.

To make the sauce, place all of the ingredients in the top of a double boiler over medium heat and stir until the chocolate has melted and the sugar has dissolved. Remove from the heat and keep warm.

To serve, halve each profiterole. Using a small ice-cream scoop, scoop out balls of ice-cream and place on the profiterole bases. Sandwich with the tops and drizzle with the sauce.

MAKES 48–50

1 litre (35 fl oz/4 cups) coffee ice-cream

PROFITEROLES

125 g (4½ oz) unsalted butter

2 teaspoons caster (superfine) sugar

185 g (6½ oz/1¼ cups) plain (all-purpose) flour

4 eggs

CHOCOLATE-ESPRESSO SAUCE

150 g (5½ oz) dark chocolate (65% cocoa solids), finely chopped

55 g (2 oz/¼ cup) caster (superfine) sugar

20 g (¾ oz) unsalted butter

125 ml (4½ fl oz/½ cup) thickened cream

125 ml (4½ fl oz/½ cup) espresso coffee

raspberry cupcakes
with white chocolate ganache

To make the ganache, place the chocolate and cream in the top of a double boiler over medium heat and stir until melted and smooth. Transfer to a bowl and refrigerate for 20 minutes. Remove and stir, then refrigerate for a further 20 minutes. Repeat the process twice more. (At this point, the ganache can be covered and refrigerated overnight.)

Meanwhile, preheat the oven to 150°C (300°F/Gas 2). Line 48 x 30 ml (1 fl oz/⅛ cup) capacity mini-muffin holes with paper cases and place 1 raspberry in the base of each.

Place the chocolate, butter, sugar and milk in the top of a double boiler over medium heat and stir until melted and smooth. Leave to cool for 15 minutes.

Sift the flour and baking powder together into a large bowl. Add the chocolate mixture and stir to combine. Add the egg and vanilla extract and mix well. The batter should be quite runny.

Transfer to a jug and pour into the cases, filling them three-quarters full. Bake for 11–12 minutes or until cooked. Cool in the tins for 3–5 minutes, then turn out onto wire racks to cool completely.

Transfer the ganache to the bowl of an electric mixer and beat on medium speed for 1–2 minutes or until soft peaks form. Transfer to a large piping bag fitted with a small star nozzle and pipe swirls of ganache onto each cupcake. Top each with a raspberry and, using a vegetable peeler, shave over curls of chocolate.

MAKES 48

48 fresh raspberries

150 g (5½ oz) white chocolate, finely chopped

120 g (4¼ oz) unsalted butter

85 g (3 oz) caster (superfine) sugar

125 ml (4½ fl oz/½ cup) milk

125 g (4½ oz) plain (all-purpose) flour

½ teaspoon baking powder

1 egg, lightly beaten

½ teaspoon natural vanilla extract

100 g (3½ oz) white chocolate, for decoration

WHITE CHOCOLATE GANACHE

180 g (6⅓ oz) white chocolate, finely chopped

400 ml (14 fl oz) pouring (single) cream

vanilla cheesecake pops
with ginger cookie crumbs

To make the cheesecake, preheat the oven to 160°C (315°F/ Gas 2–3). Line a 22 cm (8½ inch) round cake tin with baking paper. Place the cream cheese and sugar in the bowl of an electric mixer and beat on medium speed for 1–2 minutes or until smooth and combined. Add the eggs and egg yolk, one at a time, beating well after each addition. Add the sour cream, flour, vanilla seeds and ginger and combine well. Pour into the tin and bake for 1¼ hours or until just set in the centre. Leave in the tin to cool completely, then refrigerate for 3–5 hours or overnight until chilled and very firm.

Line 2 baking trays with baking paper. Using a small ice-cream scoop, scoop balls of cheesecake onto the trays. Quickly roll each in the palms of your hands and shape into a neat ball. Insert a stick into each ball and freeze for 2 hours or until very firm.

Carefully dip each cheesecake pop in the melted chocolate and tap the stick on the side of the bowl while slowly spinning to remove excess chocolate. Roll each pop in the crushed biscuit to coat well. Stand in Styrofoam to dry. Serve immediately or store in an airtight container in the refrigerator for 3–4 days.

MAKES 35–40

40 lollipop sticks

500 g (1 lb 2 oz) white chocolate, melted

125 g (4½ oz) gingersnap biscuits, crushed

VANILLA CHEESECAKE

750 g (1 lb 10 oz/3 cups) cream cheese, at room temperature

220 g (7¾ oz/1 cup) caster (superfine) sugar

3 eggs

1 egg yolk

185 g (6½ oz/¾ cup) sour cream

3 tablespoons plain (all-purpose) flour

1 vanilla bean, split and seeds scraped

45 g (1⅔ oz) candied ginger, thinly sliced

mint brownie
ice-cream sandwiches

To make the brownie, preheat the oven to 180°C (350°F/Gas 4). Grease and line 2 18 cm x 18 cm (7 inch x 7 inch) cake tins with baking paper. Place the butter and chocolate in the top of a double boiler over medium heat and stir until melted and smooth. Remove from the heat and cool slightly.

Place the sugars, eggs and mint extract in the bowl of an electric mixer and beat on medium speed for 3–5 minutes or until light and combined. Add the chocolate mixture and mix well, scraping down the sides of the bowl as required. Add the flour and beat until just combined. Divide between the tins and bake for 12–14 minutes or until still fudgy and a skewer inserted into the centre comes out with moist crumbs. Cool for 5 minutes in the tins, then remove and cool completely on wire racks.

Place the ice-cream in the refrigerator for 10 minutes or until slightly softened. Line an 18 cm x 18 cm (7 inch x 7 inch) cake tin with plastic wrap, overhanging each side by 10 cm (4 inches). Place one of the brownie slabs in the base, cover with the ice-cream in a thick layer and top with the remaining brownie slab. Cover with plastic wrap and freeze for 4–5 hours or overnight.

To serve, use the overhanging plastic wrap to lift out the brownie sandwich onto a chopping board and slice into 4 cm x 4 cm (1½ inch x 1½ inch) squares.

MAKES 16

1 litre (35 fl oz/4 cups) mint chocolate-chip ice-cream

MINT BROWNIE

125 g (4½ oz) unsalted butter

125 g (4½ oz) dark chocolate (70% cocoa solids), finely chopped

110 g (3¾ oz/½ cup) caster (superfine) sugar

95 g (3⅓ oz/½ cup lightly packed) soft brown sugar

2 eggs

1½ teaspoons natural mint extract

75 g (2¾ oz/½ cup) plain (all-purpose) flour, sifted

s'mores cupcakes

Preheat the oven to 180°C (350°F/Gas 4). Line 42 x 30 ml (1 fl oz/ ⅛ cup) capacity mini-muffin holes with paper cases.

Sift the flour, baking powder and cocoa together into a bowl.

Place the butter, sugar and vanilla extract in the bowl of an electric mixer and beat on medium speed for 2–3 minutes or until light and creamy. Add the eggs, one at a time, beating well after each addition and scraping down the sides of the bowl as required. Add the flour mixture, in 2 batches, alternating with the milk. Add the chocolate chips and mix until just combined.

Transfer the batter to a large piping bag fitted with a 3 cm (1¼ inch) plain nozzle and pipe into the cases until three-quarters full.

Bake for 10–11 minutes or until just cooked and they spring back lightly to the touch. Cool for 1–2 minutes in the tins, then turn out onto wire racks to cool completely.

To make the cookie crumbs, place all of the ingredients in a bowl and combine well. Set aside.

To make the sauce, place the chocolate, cream and butter in the top of a double boiler over medium heat and stir until melted and smooth. Leave to cool slightly.

To make the frosting, place the eggwhite, sugar and cream of tartar in the top of a double boiler over medium heat and whisk for 3 minutes or until the sugar has dissolved and the mixture is warm. Remove from the heat, add the vanilla extract and, using electric beaters, beat for 6–7 minutes or until stiff peaks form. Immediately transfer into a piping bag fitted with a 1 cm (½ inch) plain nozzle and pipe onto the cupcakes. Lightly toast the frosting with a kitchen blowtorch, then drizzle each cupcake with the sauce and sprinkle with the crumbs.

MAKES 42

180 g (6⅓ oz) plain (all-purpose) flour

1 teaspoon baking powder

30 g (1 oz/¼ cup) cocoa powder

150 g (5½ oz) unsalted butter

150 g (5½ oz) caster (superfine) sugar

1 teaspoon natural vanilla extract

3 eggs

3 tablespoons milk

50 g (1¾ oz/⅓ cup) mini milk chocolate chips

COOKIE CRUMBS

2 wheat digestive biscuits, finely crushed

¾ teaspoon caster (superfine) sugar

¼ teaspoon ground cinnamon

CHOCOLATE SAUCE

85 g (3 oz/½ cup) mini milk chocolate chips

3 tablespoons pouring (single) cream

1 teaspoon unsalted butter

MARSHMALLOW FROSTING

3 eggwhites

165 g (5¾ oz/¾ cup) caster (superfine) sugar

¼ teaspoon cream of tartar

½ teaspoon natural vanilla extract

layered jellies
with citrus and pomegranate

To make the blood orange jelly, place the juice and sugar in a small saucepan over medium heat and stir until the sugar has dissolved. Remove from the heat, add the gelatine and stir until dissolved. Cool slightly, then divide among 16 x 125 ml (4½ fl oz/½ cup) capacity jelly moulds and refrigerate for 1 hour or until set.

To make the ruby grapefruit jelly, place the juice and sugar in a small saucepan over medium heat and stir until the sugar has dissolved. Remove from the heat, add the gelatine and stir until dissolved. Cool slightly, then distribute evenly into each of the moulds and refrigerate for 1 hour or until set.

To make the pomegranate jelly, place the juice and sugar in a small saucepan over medium heat and stir until the sugar has dissolved. Remove from the heat, add the gelatine and stir until dissolved. Cool slightly, then distribute evenly into each of the moulds and refrigerate for 1 hour or until set.

To serve, unmould the jellies onto serving plates, scatter around the pomegranate seeds and garnish with the fairy floss.

MAKES 16

4 small pomegranates, seeds removed

Persian fairy floss

BLOOD ORANGE JELLY

500 ml (18 fl oz/2 cups) blood orange juice, strained

220 g (7¾ oz/1 cup) caster (superfine) sugar

1 tablespoon powdered gelatine

RUBY GRAPEFRUIT JELLY

1 litre (35 fl oz/4 cups) ruby grapefruit juice, strained

220 g (7¾ oz/1 cup) caster (superfine) sugar

2 tablespoons powdered gelatine

POMEGRANATE JELLY

500 ml (18 fl oz/2 cups) pomegranate juice, strained

165 g (5¾ oz/¾ cup) caster (superfine) sugar

1 tablespoon powdered gelatine

blood orange macarons

Line 2 baking trays with baking paper. Process the almond meal and icing sugar in a food processor until combined, then sift twice. Place the eggwhite in the bowl of an electric mixer and beat on medium speed until frothy, then increase the speed while gradually adding the caster sugar. Continue beating until stiff peaks form. Mix in the orange extract and colouring. Fold one-third into the almond mixture and combine well. Gently fold through the remaining eggwhite mixture; it should be glossy and thick, not thin and runny.

Transfer to a piping bag fitted with a 5 mm (¼ inch) plain nozzle and pipe 3 cm (1¼ inch) circles about 3 cm (1¼ inches) apart onto the trays. Leave for 1–6 hours (depending on the humidity) or until a crust forms; the macarons should no longer be sticky.

To make the curd, place the egg yolks, juices and sugar in a saucepan over medium–low heat and stir continuously for 8–9 minutes or until thick and the mixture coats a wooden spoon. Remove from the heat and add the butter, 1 cube at a time, beating well after each addition. Cover with plastic wrap and refrigerate for 1 hour.

Preheat the oven to 140°C (275°F/Gas 1). Bake the macarons for 15–18 minutes until they rise slightly. Immediately slide the macarons and paper off the trays onto wire racks to cool completely.

Transfer the curd to a piping bag fitted with a 1 cm (½ inch) plain nozzle and pipe about 1 teaspoon onto half of the macarons. Sandwich with the remaining macarons.

MAKES ABOUT 30

120 g (4¼ oz) almond meal (ground almonds)

220 g (7¾ oz) icing (confectioners') sugar

110 g (3¾ oz) eggwhite

30 g (1 oz) caster (superfine) sugar

1 teaspoon natural orange extract

orange or red food colouring, paste or powdered is preferable

BLOOD ORANGE CURD

6 egg yolks

125 ml (4½ fl oz/½ cup) blood orange juice, strained

1½ tablespoons lemon juice

165 g (5¾ oz/¾ cup) caster (superfine) sugar

80 g (2¾ oz) unsalted butter, cubed

choc-mint whoopie pies
with marshmallow frosting

Preheat the oven to 175°C (340°F/Gas 3–4). Grease and flour 2 baking trays or 3 whoopie pie tins. Sift the flour, cocoa and bicarbonate of soda together into a large bowl. Place the sugar and butter in the bowl of an electric mixer and beat on medium speed for 1–2 minutes or until light and creamy. Add the vanilla and mint extracts and egg and beat for a further minute. Reduce the speed and add the flour mixture, in 3 batches, alternating with the milk and beat until combined, scraping down the sides of the bowl as required.

Place 1½-tablespoon amounts of batter about 5 cm (2 inches) apart on the trays and bake for 8–10 minutes or until cooked through. Cool for 5 minutes on the trays, then transfer to wire racks to cool completely.

Meanwhile, to make the frosting, place the eggwhite, sugar and cream of tartar in the top of a double boiler over medium heat and whisk for 3 minutes or until warm and the sugar has dissolved. Remove from the heat, add the schnapps and, using electric beaters, beat for 6–7 minutes or until glossy and stiff peaks form.

Transfer to a piping bag fitted with a 1 cm (½ inch) plain nozzle and pipe 2 tablespoons of filling onto half of the cookies. Sandwich with the remaining cookies and roll the sides of the pies in the crushed peppermint candies to coat.

MAKES 12

150 g (5½ oz/1 cup) plain (all-purpose) flour

60 g (2¼ oz/½ cup) cocoa powder

½ teaspoon bicarbonate of soda (baking soda)

145 g (5¼ oz/⅔ cup) caster (superfine) sugar

90 g (3¼ oz) unsalted butter, at room temperature

½ teaspoon natural vanilla extract

1 teaspoon mint extract

1 egg

250 ml (9 fl oz/1 cup) milk

120 g (4¼ oz) crushed peppermint candies, for decoration

MARSHMALLOW FROSTING

3 eggwhites

165 g (5¾ oz/¾ cup) caster (superfine) sugar

¼ teaspoon cream of tartar

2 teaspoons peppermint schnapps

ginger whoopie pies
with spiced candied ginger cream

Preheat the oven to 175°C (340°F/Gas 3–4). Grease and flour 2 baking trays or 3 whoopie pie tins. Sift the flour, bicarbonate of soda, salt and ginger together into a large bowl. Place the sugars and butter in the bowl of an electric mixer and beat on medium speed for 1–2 minutes or until light and creamy. Add the vanilla extract and egg and beat for a further minute. Reduce the speed and add the flour mixture, in 3 batches, alternating with the milk and beat until combined, scraping down the sides of the bowl as required.

Place 1½-tablespoon amounts of batter about 5 cm (2 inches) apart on the trays and bake for 8–10 minutes or until cooked through. Cool for 5 minutes on the trays, then transfer to wire racks to cool completely.

Meanwhile, to make the ginger cream, place the cream cheese and butter in the bowl of an electric mixer and beat on medium speed for 2–3 minutes or until combined and smooth. Reduce the speed and add the maple syrup, icing sugar and spices and beat until combined. Fold in the candied ginger, cover with plastic wrap and refrigerate for 20 minutes or until firm.

Transfer to a piping bag fitted with a 1 cm (½ inch) plain nozzle and pipe 2 tablespoons of filling onto half of the cookies. Sandwich with the remaining cookies.

MAKES 15

260 g (9¼ oz/1¾ cups) plain (all-purpose) flour

1 teaspoon bicarbonate of soda (baking soda)

pinch of salt

1 teaspoon ground ginger

110 g (3¾ oz/½ cup) caster (superfine) sugar

95 g (3⅓ oz/½ cup lightly packed) brown sugar

125 g (4½ oz) unsalted butter, at room temperature

½ teaspoon natural vanilla extract

1 egg

250 ml (9 fl oz/1 cup) milk

**SPICED CANDIED
GINGER CREAM**

375 g (13 oz/1½ cups) cream cheese, at room temperature

75 g (2¾ oz) unsalted butter, at room temperature

2 teaspoons maple syrup

125 g (4½ oz/1 cup) icing (confectioners') sugar

1 teaspoon ground cinnamon

1 teaspoon ground nutmeg

35 g (1¼ oz) candied ginger, chopped

watermelon margarita pops
with sweet and salty lime wedges

Combine the watermelon, lime juice, agave syrup, tequila and Cointreau in a bowl and leave for 20 minutes. Transfer to a blender and pulse until juicy but with chunks of watermelon remaining.

Pour into 12 x 60 ml (2 fl oz/¼ cup) popsicle moulds. Cover with plastic wrap and insert a stick through the plastic into each pop. Freeze for 8–10 hours or until completely frozen.

To serve, place the salt and sugar on separate plates. Dip one side of each lime wedge in the salt, then the other side in the sugar. Skewer a lime wedge through the bottom of each stick.

NOTE: Agave syrup is available from health food shops.

MAKES 12

550 g (1 lb 4 oz) seedless watermelon, rind removed and cut into small chunks

40 ml (1¼ fl oz) lime juice

40 ml (1¼ fl oz) agave syrup (see note)

45 ml (1⅔ fl oz) tequila

15 ml (½ fl oz) Cointreau

12 popsicle sticks

2 tablespoons fine sea salt

2 tablespoons caster (superfine) sugar

10 lime wedges

lemon meringue cupcakes

Preheat the oven to 175°C (340°F/Gas 3–4). Line 12 x 80 ml (2½ fl oz/ ⅓ cup) capacity muffin holes with paper cases. Sift the flour and baking powder together into a bowl. Place the butter and sugar in the bowl of an electric mixer and beat for 2–3 minutes or until light and creamy. Add the eggs, one at a time, beating well after each addition. Add the flour mixture, in 3 batches, alternating with the milk and beat until combined, scraping down the sides of the bowl as required. Add the lemon extract and zest and beat to combine. Divide between the cases and bake for 18–20 minutes or until lightly golden and when a skewer inserted into the centre comes out clean. Cool in the tin for 4–5 minutes, then turn out onto wire racks to cool completely.

Using a melon baller, remove a scoop of cake from each cupcake. Fill each hole with 1–1½ tablespoons of lemon curd.

To make the meringue, place all of the ingredients in the top of a double boiler over medium heat and whisk continuously for 3–4 minutes or until the mixture is hot to the touch and reaches 50°C (122°F) on a candy thermometer. Remove the bowl and, using electric beaters, beat the mixture on high speed until glossy and stiff peaks form. Immediately cover each cupcake with meringue, using a spatula, then lightly toast with a kitchen blowtorch.

MAKES 12

185 g (6½ oz/1¼ cups) plain (all-purpose) flour

1½ teaspoons baking powder

125 g (4½ oz) unsalted butter, at room temperature

145 g (5¼ oz/⅔ cup) caster (superfine) sugar

2 eggs

125 ml (4½ fl oz/½ cup) milk

½ teaspoon natural lemon extract

1 tablespoon finely grated lemon zest

60 g (2¼ oz/¼ cup) store-bought lemon curd

MERINGUE

130 g (4¾ oz) caster (superfine) sugar

95 g (3⅓ oz) eggwhite

⅛ teaspoon salt

brownie bites
with cheesecake topping

Preheat the oven to 165°C (320°F/Gas 3). Grease and line a 27 cm x 17.5 cm (10¾ inch x 6¾ inch) slice tin with baking paper.

To make the topping, place the cream cheese and sugar in the bowl of an electric mixer and beat on medium speed for 2–3 minutes or until smooth. Add the egg, flour and vanilla extract and beat to combine. Transfer to a bowl and set aside.

Place the butter and chocolate in the top of a double boiler over medium heat and stir until melted and smooth. Place the sugar and eggs in the bowl of an electric mixer and beat for 2 minutes or until light and creamy. Add the flour, vanilla extract and salt and beat to combine.

Pour the chocolate mixture into the tin. Spoon the topping over and spread evenly. Using a butter knife, cut into the mixture to create a marbled effect. Bake for 30–35 minutes or until cooked through. Cool completely in the tin, then slice into 2.5 cm x 2.5 cm (1 inch x 1 inch) bites.

MAKES 70

125 g (4½ oz) unsalted butter

200 g (7 oz) dark chocolate (70% cocoa solids), finely chopped

220 g (7¾ oz/1 cup) caster (superfine) sugar

3 eggs

150 g (5½ oz/1 cup) plain (all-purpose) flour

1 teaspoon natural vanilla extract

¼ teaspoon salt

CHEESECAKE TOPPING

180 g (6⅓ oz) cream cheese

75 g (2¾ oz/⅓ cup) caster (superfine) sugar

1 egg

1 tablespoon plain (all-purpose) flour

1 teaspoon natural vanilla extract

glitter pops

To make the cake, preheat the oven to 180°C (350°F/Gas 4). Grease and line a 31 cm x 21 cm x 5 cm (12½ inch x 8¼ inch x 2 inch) cake tin with baking paper. Sift the flour, baking powder and salt together into a bowl. Place the butter and sugar in the bowl of an electric mixer and beat on medium speed for 2–3 minutes or until light and creamy. Add the eggs, one at a time, beating well after each addition. Add the sour cream and liqueur and mix well. Add the milk and vinegar, in 2 batches, alternating with the flour mixture, scraping down the sides of the bowl as required. Pour into the tin and bake for 35–40 minutes or until a skewer inserted into the centre comes out clean. Cool completely in the tin. Slice off the sides, top and bottom of the cake and discard. Finely crumble the remaining cake into a large bowl.

Place the butter and cream cheese in the bowl of an electric mixer and beat on medium speed for 2 minutes or until smooth. Add the icing sugar and liqueur and mix well. Add to the cake crumbs and mix well; the mixture should stick together when squeezed in your hands.

Line 2 baking trays with baking paper and roll the mixture into 30 g (1 oz) balls. Insert a stick into each ball, place on the trays and refrigerate for 30 minutes or until chilled and firm.

Carefully dip each pop in the melted chocolate, gently twirling off any excess. Sprinkle with the sanding sugar and stand in Styrofoam to dry. Serve immediately or store in an airtight container in the refrigerator for 3–4 days.

NOTE: Sanding sugar is available from specialist cake decorating shops or online.

MAKES 45–50

80 g (2¾ oz) unsalted butter, at room temperature

250 g (9 oz/1 cup) cream cheese, at room temperature

125 g (4½ oz/1 cup) icing (confectioners') sugar

2 tablespoons white chocolate liqueur

50 lollipop sticks

650 g (1 lb 7 oz) white chocolate, melted

75 g (2¾ oz/⅓ cup) gold sanding sugar (see note)

WHITE CHOCOLATE CAKE

300 g (10½ oz/2 cups) plain (all-purpose) flour

2 teaspoons baking powder

¼ teaspoon salt

225 g (8 oz) unsalted butter, at room temperature

440 g (15½ oz/2 cups) caster (superfine) sugar

4 eggs

85 g (3 oz/⅓ cup) sour cream

65 ml (2¼ fl oz) white chocolate liqueur

65 ml (2¼ fl oz) milk

1 tablespoon white vinegar

gingersnap and peach
ice-cream sandwiches

To make the cookies, preheat the oven to 180°C (350°F/Gas 4). Line 2 baking trays with baking paper. Sift the flour, bicarbonate of soda, spices and salt together into a bowl. Place the butter and caster sugar in the bowl of an electric mixer and beat on medium speed for 2–3 minutes or until light and creamy. Add the egg and molasses and mix well. Add the flour mixture and gingers and mix well, scraping down the sides of the bowl.

Roll the dough into 15 g (½ oz) balls. Roll each in the raw sugar, place 3 cm–5 cm (1¼ inches–2 inches) apart on the trays and flatten with the base of a glass dipped in raw sugar. Bake for 7–9 minutes or until crisp. Cool completely on the trays. Use immediately or store in an airtight container for up to 4 days.

Line 2 baking trays with baking paper. Use a small ice-cream scoop or melon baller to scoop out 30 balls of ice-cream, place on the trays and refrigerate for 2–3 minutes or until slightly softened. Place the balls on half of the cookies and sandwich with the remaining cookies. Place in the freezer until ready to serve.

NOTE: Golden caster sugar is available from gourmet food shops. Blackstrap molasses is available from health food shops. To make slightly larger ice-cream sandwiches, roll the dough into 30 g (1 oz) balls and bake for 12–15 minutes; makes 15 sandwiches. Alternatively, roll the mixture into 20 g (¾ oz) balls and bake for 10–12 minutes; makes 20 sandwiches.

MAKES 30

1.5 litres (52 fl oz/6 cups) peach ice-cream

GINGERSNAP COOKIES

300 g (10½ oz/2 cups) plain (all-purpose) flour

1½ teaspoons bicarbonate of soda (baking soda)

2 teaspoons ground cinnamon

1 teaspoon ground allspice

½ teaspoon salt

125 g (4½ oz) unsalted butter, at room temperature

220 g (7¾ oz/1 cup) golden caster (superfine) sugar (see note)

1 egg, lightly beaten

85 ml (4 fl oz/¼ cup) unsulphured blackstrap molasses (see note)

2 teaspoons freshly grated ginger

½ cup minced candied ginger

140 g (5 oz/⅔ cup) raw (demerara) sugar

chocolate indulgence
ice-cream sandwiches

To make the cookies, preheat the oven to 175°C (340°F/Gas 3–4). Line 2 baking trays with baking paper. Sift together the flour, baking powder and cocoa. Place the butter, sugar and vanilla extract in the bowl of an electric mixer and beat on medium speed for 1–2 minutes or until light and creamy. Add the egg and mix well. Add the flour mixture and mix well. Stir in the chocolate chips.

Roll the dough into 20 g (¾ oz) balls and place on the trays 3 cm–5 cm (1¼ inches–2 inches) apart. Flatten each with the palm of your hand or the base of a floured glass. Bake for 7 minutes or until fragrant. Cool for 2 minutes on the trays, then remove to wire racks and cool completely. Use immediately or store in an airtight container for up to 4 days.

Line 2 baking trays with baking paper. Use a small ice-cream scoop or melon baller to scoop out 20 balls of ice-cream, place on the trays and refrigerate for 2–3 minutes or until slightly softened. Place the balls on half of the cookies, then sandwich with the remaining cookies. Place on the trays and freeze until firm.

Working with one sandwich at a time, carefully dip half a sandwich in the melted chocolate and place on the tray. Repeat with the remaining balls and cookies. Place in the freezer until ready to serve.

NOTE: To make slightly larger ice-cream sandwiches, roll the mixture into 25 g (1 oz) balls and bake for 8–9 minutes; makes 15 sandwiches. Alternatively, roll the mixture into 30 g (1 oz) balls and bake for 10–11 minutes; makes 13 sandwiches.

MAKES 20

1 litre (35 fl oz/4 cups) chocolate ice-cream

225 g (8 oz) dark chocolate (70% cocoa solids), melted

CHOCOLATE CHIP COOKIES

150 g (5½ oz/1 cup) plain (all-purpose) flour, plus 2 tablespoons extra

1 teaspoon baking powder

40 g (1½ oz/⅓ cup) cocoa powder

125 g (4½ oz) unsalted butter, at room temperature

165 g (5¾ oz/¾ cup) caster (superfine) sugar

1 teaspoon natural vanilla extract

1 egg

120 g (4¼ oz/¾ cup) mini milk chocolate chips

120 g (4¼ oz/¾ cup) mini dark chocolate chips

banana daiquiri cupcakes

Preheat the oven to 180°C (350°F/Gas 4). Line 36 x 30 ml (1 fl oz/⅛ cup) capacity mini-muffin holes with paper cases.

Sift the flour, bicarbonate of soda and baking powder together into a bowl. Combine the banana, buttermilk and rum. Place the butter and sugar in the bowl of an electric mixer and beat on medium speed for 2–3 minutes or until light and creamy. Add the egg and beat well. Add the banana mixture, in 3 batches, alternating with the flour mixture, scraping down the sides of the bowl as required.

Transfer the batter to a large piping bag fitted with a 1 cm (½ inch) plain nozzle and pipe into the cases, filling them three-quarters full. Bake for 10 minutes or until lightly golden and they spring back lightly to the touch. Cool in the tins for 1–2 minutes, then turn out onto wire racks to cool completely.

To make the frosting, place the eggwhite, sugar, glucose and 2 tablespoons water in the top of a double boiler over medium heat and, using electric beaters, beat for 7–8 minutes or until glossy and stiff. Add the rum and coconut extract and beat for a further minute. Immediately frost the cupcakes and top with the shredded coconut.

MAKES 36

150 g (5½ oz/1 cup) plain (all-purpose) flour

½ teaspoon bicarbonate of soda (baking soda)

¼ teaspoon baking powder

175 g (6 oz/about 2) mashed banana

3 tablespoons buttermilk

30 ml (1 fl oz) dark rum

65 g (2⅓ oz) unsalted butter, at room temperature

95 g (3⅓ oz/½ cup lightly packed) soft brown sugar

1 egg

COCONUT AND RUM FROSTING`

2 eggwhites

110 g (3¾ oz/½ cup) caster (superfine) sugar

3 tablespoons glucose syrup

40 ml (1¼ fl oz) dark rum

1 teaspoon natural coconut extract

30 g (1 oz/½ cup) shredded coconut, toasted (optional)

chocolate macarons
with espresso and cocoa nibs

Line 2 baking trays with baking paper. Process the almond meal, cocoa and icing sugar in a food processor until combined, then sift twice. Place the eggwhite in the bowl of an electric mixer and beat on medium speed until frothy, then increase the speed while gradually adding the caster sugar. Continue beating until stiff peaks form. Fold one-third into the almond mixture and combine well. Gently fold through the remaining eggwhite mixture; it should be glossy and thick, not thin and runny.

Transfer to a piping bag fitted with a 5 mm (¼ inch) plain nozzle and pipe 3 cm (1¼ inch) circles about 3 cm (1¼ inches) apart onto the trays. Leave at room temperature for 1–6 hours (depending on the humidity) or until a crust forms; the macarons should no longer be sticky to the touch.

Preheat the oven to 140°C (275°F/Gas 1). Bake the macarons for 15–18 minutes until they rise slightly. Immediately slide the macarons and paper off the trays onto wire racks to cool completely.

Meanwhile, to make the ganache, place the cream and coffee granules in the top of a double boiler over medium heat and stir until the coffee has dissolved. Add the chocolate and stir until melted and smooth. Refrigerate for 20–25 minutes or until firm but pliable, then gently stir through the cocoa nibs.

Transfer to a small piping bag fitted with a 1 cm (½ inch) plain nozzle and pipe about 1 teaspoon onto half of the macarons. Sandwich with the remaining macarons.

NOTE: Cocoa nibs are available from gourmet food shops.

MAKES ABOUT 30

110 g (3¾ oz) almond meal (ground almonds)

15 g (½ oz) cocoa powder

200 g (7 oz) icing (confectioners') sugar

110 g (3¾ oz) eggwhite

30 g (1 oz) caster (superfine) sugar

ESPRESSO GANACHE

80 ml (2½ fl oz/⅓ cup) pouring (single) cream

2 teaspoons instant coffee granules

120 g (4¼ oz) dark chocolate (70% cocoa solids), chopped

2 tablespoons cocoa nibs (see note)

lemon madeleines
with limoncello glaze

Preheat the oven to 180°C (350°F/Gas 4). Grease 2 madeleine tins.

Sift the flour and baking powder together into a bowl. Place the eggs, sugar and lemon zest and extract in the bowl of an electric mixer and whisk on medium–high speed for 4–5 minutes or until pale and thickened. Gently fold in the flour mixture. Fold in the butter, a little at a time, folding well after each addition. Leave to rest for 15–20 minutes.

Meanwhile, to make the glaze, whisk all of the ingredients in a bowl until combined and smooth. Set aside.

Fill the tins with the madeleine mixture until three-quarters full and bake for 7–9 minutes or until the edges are light golden. Turn out onto wire racks and cool for 2–3 minutes, then spoon over the glaze to coat.

Repeat with the remaining batter. Madeleines are best eaten on the day of making.

MAKES 48

130 g (4¾ oz) plain (all-purpose) flour

½ teaspoon baking powder

3 eggs

130 g (4¾ oz) caster (superfine) sugar

2 tablespoons finely grated lemon zest

1 teaspoon natural lemon extract

115 g (4 oz) unsalted butter, melted

LIMONCELLO GLAZE

190 g (6¾ oz/1½ cups) icing (confectioners') sugar

2 tablespoons lemon juice

40 ml (1¼ fl oz) limoncello

double chocolate
whoopie pies

Preheat the oven to 175°C (340°F/Gas 3–4). Grease and flour 2 baking trays or 3 whoopie pie tins. Sift the flour, cocoa and bicarbonate of soda together into a large bowl. Place the sugar and butter in the bowl of an electric mixer and beat on medium speed for 2–3 minutes or until light and creamy. Add the vanilla extract and egg and beat for a further minute. Reduce the speed and add the flour mixture, in 3 batches, alternating with the milk and beat until combined, scraping down the sides of the bowl as required.

Place 1½-tablespoon amounts of batter about 5 cm (2 inches) apart on the trays and bake for 8–10 minutes or until cooked through. Cool for 5 minutes on the trays, then transfer to wire racks to cool completely.

Meanwhile, to make the buttercream, place the eggwhite and sugar in the top of a double boiler over medium heat and whisk for 3–4 minutes or until warm and the sugar has dissolved. Remove from the heat. Using electric beaters, beat the mixture on medium–high speed for 6–7 minutes or until glossy and stiff peaks form. Reduce the speed and add the butter, 1 cube at a time, beating well after each addition. Continue to beat for 2–3 minutes. Combine the melted chocolate and cocoa. Add to the eggwhite mixture and beat to combine.

Transfer to a piping bag fitted with a 1 cm (½ inch) plain nozzle and pipe 2 tablespoons of filling onto half of the cookies. Sandwich with the remaining cookies.

MAKES 12

150 g (5½ oz/1 cup) plain (all-purpose) flour

60 g (2¼ oz/½ cup) cocoa powder

½ teaspoon bicarbonate of soda (baking soda)

145 g (5¼ oz/⅔ cup) caster (superfine) sugar

90 g (3¼ oz) unsalted butter, at room temperature

1 teaspoon natural vanilla extract

1 egg

250 ml (9 fl oz/1 cup) milk

CHOCOLATE BUTTERCREAM

3 eggwhites

145 g (5¼ oz/⅔ cup) caster (superfine) sugar

160 g (5⅔ oz) unsalted butter, cubed and at room temperature

125 g (4½ oz) dark chocolate (65% cocoa solids), melted

2 tablespoons cocoa powder

g & t pops

Place the lemon and lime juices, sugar and lime slices in a non-reactive saucepan over medium heat and simmer for 1–2 minutes or until the sugar has dissolved. Remove from the heat and leave to cool for 5 minutes.

Add the tonic and gin to the lemon syrup and stir to combine. Pour into 10 x 60 ml (2 fl oz/¼ cup) popsicle moulds and add a lime slice to each. Cover with plastic wrap and insert a stick through the plastic into each pop. Freeze for 8–10 hours or until completely frozen.

MAKES 10

85 ml (2¾ fl oz) lemon juice

60 ml (2 fl oz/¼ cup) lime juice

165 g (5¾ oz/¾ cup) caster (superfine) sugar

10 small lime or lemon slices

300 ml (10½ fl oz) tonic water

65 ml (2¼ fl oz) gin

10 popsicle sticks

pimm's pops

Place all of the ingredients, except the sticks, in a large measuring jug and refrigerate for 1–2 hours to infuse.

Pour the Pimm's mixture into 10 x 60 ml (2 fl oz/¼ cup) capacity popsicle moulds and add a mint leaf, piece of fruit or slice of cucumber to each popsicle. Cover with plastic wrap and insert a stick through the plastic into each pop. Freeze for 8–10 hours or until completely frozen.

MAKES 10

250 ml (9 fl oz/1 cup) ginger ale

250 ml (9 fl oz/1 cup) lemonade

185 ml (6 fl oz/¾ cup) Pimm's

8 mint leaves

2 orange slices

2 lemon slices

4 small cucumber slices

4 strawberries, halved

10 popsicle sticks

persian rose macarons

Line 2 baking trays with baking paper. Process the almond meal, pistachios and icing sugar in a food processor until the pistachios are finely chopped, then sift twice. Place the eggwhite in the bowl of an electric mixer and beat on medium speed until frothy, then increase the speed while gradually adding the caster sugar. Beat until stiff peaks form. Mix in enough colouring for desired effect. Fold one-third into the almond mixture and combine well. Gently fold through the remaining eggwhite mixture; it should be glossy and thick, not thin and runny.

Transfer to a piping bag fitted with a 5 mm (¼ inch) plain nozzle and pipe 3 cm (1¼ inch) circles about 3 cm (1¼ inches) apart onto the trays. Leave at room temperature for 1–6 hours (depending on the humidity) or until a crust forms; the macarons should no longer be sticky to the touch.

Preheat the oven to 140°C (275°F/Gas 1). Bake the macarons for 15–18 minutes until they rise slightly. Immediately slide the macarons and paper off the trays onto wire racks to cool completely.

To make the buttercream, place the sugar and eggwhite in the top of a double boiler over medium heat and whisk for 3–4 minutes or until warm and the sugar has dissolved. Remove from the heat. Using electric beaters, beat the mixture on medium–high speed for 6–7 minutes or until glossy and stiff peaks form. Reduce the speed and add the butter, 1 cube at a time, beating well after each addition. Mix in the rosewater and enough colouring for desired effect.

Transfer to a piping bag fitted with a 1 cm (½ inch) plain nozzle and pipe about 1 teaspoon onto half of the macarons. Sandwich with the remaining macarons.

MAKES ABOUT 30

80 g (2¾ oz/¾ cup) almond meal
(ground almonds)

40 g (1½ oz) pistachio kernels

220 g (7¾ oz) icing (confectioners')
sugar

110 g (3¾ oz) eggwhite

30 g (1 oz) caster (superfine) sugar

green food colouring, paste or powdered
is preferable

ROSE BUTTERCREAM

100 g (3½ oz) caster (superfine) sugar

2 eggwhites

185 g (6½ oz) unsalted butter, cubed
and at room temperature

3 teaspoons rosewater

pink food colouring, paste or powdered
is preferable

black velvet whoopie pies

Preheat the oven to 175°C (340°F/Gas 3–4). Grease and flour 2 baking trays or 3 whoopie pie tins. Sift the flour, cocoa, bicarbonate of soda and salt together into a large bowl. Place the sugar and butter in the bowl of an electric mixer and beat on medium speed for 1–2 minutes or until light and creamy. Add the vanilla extract and egg and beat for a further minute. Reduce the speed and add the flour mixture, in 3 batches, alternating with the buttermilk and beat until just combined, then beat in the vinegar, scraping down the sides of the bowl as required.

Place 1½-tablespoon amounts of batter about 5 cm (2 inches) apart on the trays and bake for 8–10 minutes or until cooked through. Cool for 5 minutes on the trays, then transfer to wire racks to cool completely.

Meanwhile, to make the frosting, place the cream cheese, butter and vanilla extract in the bowl of an electric mixer and beat on medium–high speed for 2–3 minutes or until combined and smooth. Reduce the speed, add the icing sugar and beat until combined. Cover with plastic wrap and refrigerate for 20–25 minutes or until firm.

Transfer to a piping bag fitted with a 1 cm (½ inch) plain nozzle and pipe 2 tablespoons of filling onto half of the cookies. Sandwich with the remaining cookies.

MAKES 15

225 g (8 oz/1½ cups) plain (all-purpose) flour

60 g (2¼ oz/½ cup) cocoa powder

1 teaspoon bicarbonate of soda (baking soda)

pinch of salt

160 g (5⅔ oz/1 cup) brown sugar

125 g (4½ oz) unsalted butter, at room temperature

1 teaspoon natural vanilla extract

1 egg

250 ml (9 fl oz/1 cup) buttermilk

½ teaspoon white vinegar

CREAM CHEESE FROSTING

375 g (13 oz/1½ cups) cream cheese, at room temperature

75 g (2¾ oz) unsalted butter, at room temperature

1 teaspoon natural vanilla extract

125 g (4½ oz/1 cup) icing (confectioners') sugar, sifted

walnut brownie pops

To make the brownie, preheat the oven to 175°C (340°F/Gas 3–4). Grease and line a 31 cm x 21 cm x 5 cm (12½ inch x 8¼ inch x 2 inch) cake tin with baking paper. Place the chocolate and butter in the top of a double boiler over medium heat and stir until melted and smooth. Add the sugars and stir until dissolved. Remove from the heat and cool slightly. Add the egg and vanilla extract and stir to combine. Sift the flour and cocoa together into a large bowl, add the chocolate mixture, combine well and stir in the walnuts.

Pour into the tin and bake for 25–30 minutes or until still fudgy and a skewer inserted into the centre comes out with moist crumbs. Cool completely in the tin.

Line 2 baking trays with baking paper. Using a small ice-cream scoop, scoop out balls of brownie onto the trays. Quickly roll each in the palms of your hands to shape into a neat ball. Insert a stick into each ball and refrigerate for 2 hours or until well chilled and firm.

Carefully dip each brownie pop in the melted chocolate and tap the stick on the side of the bowl while slowly spinning to remove excess chocolate. Roll each pop in the sprinkles to coat well. Stand in Styrofoam to dry. Serve immediately or store in an airtight container in the refrigerator for 3–4 days.

40 lollipop sticks

500 g (1 lb 2 oz) dark chocolate (70% cocoa solids), melted

chocolate sprinkles, for coating

WALNUT BROWNIE

300 g (10½ oz) dark chocolate (70% cocoa solids), finely chopped

185 g (6½ oz) unsalted butter, at room temperature

330 g (11¾ oz/1½ cups) caster (superfine) sugar

45 g (1¾ oz/¼ cup lightly packed) soft brown sugar

4 eggs, lightly beaten

2 teaspoons natural vanilla extract

150 g (5½ oz/1 cup) plain (all-purpose) flour

2 tablespoons cocoa powder

100 g (3½ oz/1 cup) walnuts, finely chopped

tangerine mimosa jellies

Place the juice, wine and sugar in a saucepan over medium–low heat and bring to a simmer, stirring until the sugar has dissolved. Remove from the heat.

Add the gelatine and stir until dissolved. Cool to room temperature, then pour into 12 Champagne glasses and refrigerate for 2–3 hours or until set.

To serve, garnish with the fairy floss.

MAKES 12

400 ml (14 fl oz) tangerine juice, strained

1.1 litres (38½ fl oz) sparkling white wine

400 g (14 oz) caster (superfine) sugar

2 tablespoons powdered gelatine

Persian fairy floss, to garnish

passionfruit macarons

Line 2 baking trays with baking paper. Process the almond meal and icing sugar in a food processor until combined, then sift twice. Place the eggwhite in the bowl of an electric mixer and beat on medium speed until frothy, then increase the speed while gradually adding the caster sugar. Continue beating until stiff peaks form. Mix in enough colouring for desired effect. Fold one-third into the almond mixture and combine well. Gently fold through the remaining eggwhite mixture; it should be glossy and thick, not thin and runny.

Transfer to a piping bag fitted with a 5 mm (¼ inch) plain nozzle and pipe 3 cm (1¼ inch) circles about 3 cm (1¼ inches) apart onto the trays. Leave for 1–6 hours (depending on the humidity) or until a crust forms; the macarons should no longer be sticky.

To make the curd, place the egg yolks, sugar, pulp and lemon juice in a saucepan over medium–low heat and, using a wooden spoon, stir continuously for 8–9 minutes or until thick and the mixture coats the spoon. Remove from the heat and add the butter, 1 cube at a time, beating well after each addition. Cover with plastic wrap and refrigerate for 1 hour.

Preheat the oven to 140°C (275°F/Gas 1). Bake the macarons for 15–18 minutes until they rise slightly. Immediately slide the macarons and paper off the trays onto wire racks to cool completely.

Transfer the curd to a piping bag fitted with a 1 cm (½ inch) plain nozzle and pipe about 1 teaspoon onto half of the macarons. Sandwich with the remaining macarons.

MAKES ABOUT 30

120 g (4¼ oz) almond meal (ground almonds)

220 g (7¾ oz) icing (confectioners') sugar

110 g (3¾ oz) eggwhite

30 g (1 oz) caster (superfine) sugar

yellow food colouring, paste or powdered is preferable

PASSIONFRUIT CURD

5 egg yolks

165 g (5¾ oz/¾ cup) caster (superfine) sugar

125 ml (4½ fl oz/½ cup) passionfruit pulp

1 tablespoon lemon juice

80 g (2¾ oz) unsalted butter, cubed

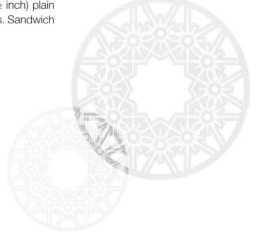

peanut macarons
with salted caramel

Line 2 baking trays with baking paper. Process the almond meal, peanuts and icing sugar in a food processor until the peanuts are finely chopped, then sift twice. Place the eggwhite in the bowl of an electric mixer and beat on medium speed until frothy, then increase the speed while gradually adding the caster sugar. Beat until stiff peaks form. Fold one-third into the almond mixture and combine well. Gently fold through the remaining eggwhite mixture; it should be glossy and thick.

Transfer to a piping bag fitted with a 5 mm (¼ inch) nozzle and pipe 3 cm (1¼ inch) circles about 3 cm (1¼ inches) apart onto the trays. Leave for 1–6 hours or until a crust forms; the macarons should no longer be sticky.

Preheat the oven to 140°C (275°F/Gas 1). Bake the macarons for 15–18 minutes until they rise slightly. Immediately slide the macarons and paper off the trays onto wire racks to cool completely.

To make the filling, place the sugar, glucose and 1½ tablespoons water in a saucepan over medium–high heat, swirling the pan (do not stir) to dissolve the sugar. Increase the heat to high, bring to the boil and cook until golden. Remove from the heat and carefully add the cream. Place over low heat, add the butter, 1 cube at a time, beating well after each addition. Mix in the salt. Leave to cool until thickened.

Transfer to a piping bag fitted with a 1 cm (½ inch) nozzle and pipe about 1 teaspoon onto half of the macarons. Sandwich with the remaining macarons.

MAKES ABOUT 30

80 g (2¾ oz/¾ cup) almond meal (ground almonds)

40 g (1½ oz) roasted peanuts

220 g (7¾ oz) icing (confectioners') sugar

110 g (3¾ oz) eggwhite

30 g (1 oz) caster (superfine) sugar

SALTED CARAMEL FILLING

110 g (3¾ oz/½ cup) caster (superfine) sugar

2 teaspoons glucose syrup

3 tablespoons pouring (single) cream

60 g (2¼ oz) butter, cubed and at room temperature

¼ teaspoon fleur de sel or fine sea salt flakes

ice-cream cake pops

To make the cake, preheat the oven to 180°C (350°F/Gas 4). Grease and line a 22 cm (8½ inch) round cake tin with baking paper. Sift the flour and cocoa together into a large bowl. Combine the sugar and 125 ml (4½ fl oz/½ cup) boiling water in the top of a double boiler over medium heat and stir until dissolved. Add the butter and chopped chocolate and stir until melted and smooth. Cool slightly. Combine the egg and vanilla extract, add to the flour mixture and mix well. Add the chocolate mixture and mix well. Pour into the tin and bake for 30–35 minutes or until a skewer inserted into the centre comes out clean. Remove from the tin and cool completely on a wire rack. Finely crumble the cake into a large bowl.

Place the butter, icing sugar and cocoa in the bowl of an electric mixer and beat for 1–2 minutes or until light and creamy. Add the cream and mix well. Add to the cake crumbs and, using your hands, mix well; the mixture should stick together when squeezed.

Line 2 baking trays with baking paper. Roll the mixture into 30 g (1 oz) balls. Press each onto an ice-cream cone and freeze for 15 minutes or until firm.

Carefully dip each pop in the melted dark chocolate, gently twirling off excess. Stand in Styrofoam to dry. Using a teaspoon, drip some white chocolate over the dark chocolate and coat with the sprinkles. Serve immediately or store in an airtight container in the refrigerator for up to 3–4 days.

80 g (2¾ oz) unsalted butter, at room temperature

125 g (4½ oz/1 cup) icing (confectioners') sugar

2 tablespoons cocoa powder

2 tablespoons pouring (single) cream

500 g (1 lb 2 oz) dark chocolate (65% cocoa solids), finely chopped

30 mini waffle ice-cream cones

500 g (1 lb 2 oz) dark chocolate (65% cocoa solids), melted

200 g (7 oz) white chocolate, melted

sprinkles, to decorate

CHOCOLATE CAKE

110 g (3¾ oz) self-raising (self-rising) flour

40 g (1½ oz/⅓ cup) cocoa powder

200 g (7 oz) caster (superfine) sugar

80 g (2¾ oz) unsalted butter, at room temperature

125 g (4½ oz) dark chocolate (65% cocoa solids), finely chopped

2 eggs, lightly beaten

1 teaspoon natural vanilla extract

meyer lemon bars

Preheat the oven to 180°C (350°F/Gas 4).

To make the crust, place the flour and sugar in the bowl of a food processor and pulse to combine. Add the butter, 1 piece at a time, until the mixture resembles pea-sized crumbs.

Press the mixture into the base of a 23.5 cm x 33.5 cm (9¼ inch x 13¼ inch) slice tin. Bake for 18–20 minutes or until golden. Cool in the tin for 20–30 minutes.

Reduce the temperature to 150°C (300°F/Gas 2). Whisk the eggs, sugar, flour and lemon juice together in a bowl until combined and smooth. Stir in the zest and pour over the crust. Bake for 25–30 minutes or until set. Remove from the oven and cool completely on a wire rack. Dust with the extra icing sugar and cut into 6 cm x 2.5 cm (2½ x 1 inch) bars.

NOTE: Meyer lemons are available in the cooler months from select greengrocers and farmers' markets.

MAKES 25

6 eggs

550 g (1 lb 4 oz/2½ cups) caster (superfine) sugar

75 g (2¾ oz/½ cup) plain (all-purpose) flour

250 ml (9 fl oz/1 cup) meyer lemon juice, strained (see note)

3 tablespoons finely grated meyer lemon zest

SWEET CRUST

225 g (8 oz/1½ cups) plain (all-purpose) flour

65 g (2⅓ oz/½ cup) icing (confectioners') sugar, plus extra for dusting

180 g (6⅓ oz) unsalted butter, cut into 10 pieces

blueberry mojito
popsicles

Place the sugar, mint, blueberries, lime juice and 3 tablespoons water in a saucepan over medium heat and simmer for 1–2 minutes or until the sugar has dissolved. Remove from the heat and leave to cool for 5 minutes to infuse.

Add the rum and soda to the blueberry syrup and stir to combine. Pour into 12 x 60 ml (2 fl oz/¼ cup) capacity popsicle moulds. Cover with plastic wrap and insert a stick through the plastic into each pop. Freeze for 8–10 hours or until completely frozen.

MAKES 12

110 g (3¾ oz/½ cup) golden caster (superfine) sugar

¼ cup chopped mint

115 g (4 oz/¾ cup) fresh blueberries

3 tablespoons lime juice

75 ml (2⅓ fl oz) rum

300 ml (10½ fl oz) soda water

12 popsicle sticks

strawberry tartlets
with sticky balsamic glaze

To make the pastry, place the butter and icing sugar in the bowl of an electric mixer and beat for 2–3 minutes or until light and creamy. Add the egg yolk and vanilla seeds and beat to combine well. Add the flour and beat until just combined. Turn the dough out onto a floured surface, shape into a disc, wrap in plastic wrap and refrigerate for 1–2 hours.

Preheat the oven to 180°C (350°F/Gas 4).

Meanwhile, to make the glaze, place the vinegar and honey in a saucepan over medium heat and simmer until reduced by one-third and the mixture is thick and syrupy. Cool completely.

Roll the dough into 50 x 8 g (¼ oz) balls. Place each ball in a 3.5 cm (1¼ inch) fluted tartlet tin and press the pastry into the base and sides. Freeze for 10 minutes.

Place the pastry cases on baking trays and bake for 7–9 minutes or until golden and cooked. If the pastry puffs up, use a teaspoon to gently push it down. Cool in the tins for 8–10 minutes, then turn out onto wire racks and cool completely.

To serve, combine the goat's curd, ricotta, honey and orange zest in a bowl. Transfer to a large piping bag fitted with a 5 mm (¼ inch) plain nozzle and pipe the mixture into the cases. Top each with a strawberry half and drizzle with the balsamic glaze.

MAKES ABOUT 50

300 g (10½ oz) goat's curd

200 g (7 oz) ricotta

3 teaspoons orange blossom honey

1 teaspoon finely grated orange zest

25 strawberries, halved

VANILLA SHORTCRUST PASTRY

125 g (4½ oz) unsalted butter, at room temperature

80 g (2¾ oz) icing (confectioners') sugar

1 egg yolk

½ vanilla bean, split and seeds scraped

200 g (7 oz/1⅓ cups) plain (all-purpose) flour, sifted

BALSAMIC GLAZE

125 ml (4½ fl oz/½ cup) good-quality balsamic vinegar

115 g (4 oz/⅓ cup) honey

persian florentines

Preheat the oven to 175°C (340°F/Gas 3–4). Line 2 baking trays with baking paper.

Place the orange peel, cherries, nuts, orange blossom water and flour in a bowl and stir to combine.

Place the butter, sugar, honey and cream in a saucepan over medium heat, bring to the boil and cook until it reaches 112°C (234°F; soft-ball stage) on a candy thermometer. Add to the fruit and nut mixture and stir to combine.

Drop 1-tablespoon amounts of mixture about 5 cm (2 inches) apart on the trays and flatten slightly. Bake for 12–14 minutes or until golden and set. Cool on the trays completely.

Place the melted chocolate in a small piping bag fitted with a 5 mm (¼ inch) plain nozzle and pipe stripes across each cookie. Leave to set. Store in an airtight container for up to 1 week.

MAKES 20

35 g (1¼ oz) chopped candied orange peel

100 g (3½ oz) dried sour cherries

80 g (2¾ oz) flaked almonds

65 g (2⅓ oz) pistachio kernels, chopped

1¼ teaspoons orange blossom water

35 g (1¼ oz/¼ cup) plain (all-purpose) flour

40 g (1½ oz) unsalted butter

60 g (2¼ oz) caster (superfine) sugar

60 g (2¼ oz) honey

80 ml (2½ fl oz/⅓ cup) pouring (single) cream

85 g (3 oz) dark chocolate (70% cocoa solids), melted

almond corkscrews

Preheat the oven to 180°C (350°F/Gas 4). Line 2 baking trays with baking paper.

Place the butter and sugar in the bowl of an electric mixer and beat on medium speed for 2–3 minutes or until light and fluffy. Gradually add the eggwhite and almond extract and beat well until combined. Add the flour and beat to combine.

Transfer to a large piping bag fitted with a 5 mm (¼ inch) plain nozzle. Pipe six 7 cm–8 cm (2¾ inch–3¼ inch) long lines about 5 cm (2 inches) apart onto one tray. Only prepare one tray of cookies to bake at a time. Scatter the lines with one-third of the almonds and bake for 4–5 minutes or until the edges begin to turn golden.

Remove from the oven. Working quickly, lift a cookie off the tray, using a spatula, then wrap it around the handle of a wooden spoon and leave to cool. Repeat with the remaining cookies. If the cookies cool and harden before being shaped, warm in the oven for 1 minute to soften. Slide the cooled corkscrews off the spoons.

Repeat the process with the remaining mixture, piping lines onto a cool baking tray each time. Store the corkscrews in an airtight container for 4 days.

MAKES 36

60 g (2¼ oz) unsalted butter, at room temperature

90 g (3¼ oz) caster (superfine) sugar

2 eggwhites, lightly beaten, at room temperature

1 teaspoon natural almond extract

50 g (1¾ oz/⅓ cup) plain (all-purpose) flour

65 g (2⅓ oz/¾ cup) toasted flaked almonds

spiced pumpkin whoopie
pies with pecan mascarpone

Preheat the oven to 175°C (340°F/Gas 3–4). Grease and flour 2 baking trays or 3 whoopie pie tins. Sift the flour, spices, bicarbonate of soda and baking powder together into a large bowl. Place the sugar and butter in the bowl of an electric mixer and beat on medium speed for 1–2 minutes or until light and creamy. Add the egg, pumpkin and vanilla extract and beat to combine well. Reduce the speed and add the flour mixture, in 3 batches, alternating with the milk and beat until combined, scraping down the sides of the bowl as required.

Place 1½-tablespoon amounts of batter about 5 cm (2 inches) apart on the trays and bake for 9–12 minutes or until cooked through. Cool for 5 minutes on the trays, then transfer to wire racks to cool completely.

To make the pecan mascarpone, whisk the cream until soft peaks form. Place the mascarpone and vanilla extract in the bowl of an electric mixer and beat on medium speed for 1–2 minutes or until combined and smooth. Reduce the speed, add the icing sugar and nutmeg and beat until combined. Fold in the whipped cream and the pecans. Cover with plastic wrap and refrigerate for 20 minutes or until firm.

Transfer to a piping bag fitted with a 1 cm (½ inch) plain nozzle and pipe 2 tablespoons of filling onto half of the cookies. Sandwich with the remaining cookies.

NOTE: To make pumpkin purée, roast the pumpkin in a preheated 200°C (400°F/Gas 6) oven until tender, then process in a food processor until it becomes a smooth purée. Cool.

MAKES 16

150 g (5½ oz/1 cup) plain (all-purpose) flour

1 teaspoon ground cinnamon

½ teaspoon ground nutmeg

¼ teaspoon ground cloves

½ teaspoon bicarbonate of soda (baking soda)

½ teaspoon baking powder

185 g (6½ oz/1 cup lightly packed) soft brown sugar

125 g (4½ oz) unsalted butter, at room temperature

1 egg

250 g (9 oz/1 cup) pumpkin purée (see note)

½ teaspoon natural vanilla extract

125 ml (4½ fl oz/½ cup) milk

PECAN MASCARPONE

250 ml (9 fl oz/1 cup) pouring (single) cream

300 g (10½ oz) marscarpone, at room temperature

1 teaspoon natural vanilla extract

125 g (4½ oz/1 cup) icing (confectioners') sugar, sifted

½ teaspoon ground nutmeg

35 g (1¼ oz/⅓ cup) roasted pecans, chopped

hibiscus vodka pops

Place the hibiscus flowers or tea bags in a heatproof jug, add 500 ml (18 fl oz/2 cups) boiling water and leave for 15 minutes to infuse.

Remove the flowers or tea bags, add the agave syrup and stir until dissolved. Add the vodka and leave to cool slightly.

Pour into 10 x 60 ml (2 fl oz/¼ cup) capacity popsicle moulds. Cover with plastic wrap and insert a stick through the plastic into each pop. Freeze for 8–10 hours or until completely frozen.

NOTE: Dried hibiscus flowers and agave syrup are available from health food shops.

MAKES 10

12 g (½ oz/¼ cup) dried hibiscus flowers or 3 hibiscus tea bags (see note)

60 ml (2 fl oz/¼ cup) agave syrup (see note)

60 ml (2 fl oz/¼ cup) vodka

10 popsicle sticks

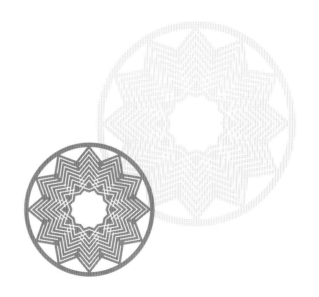

chocolate tarts
with raspberry

Place the chocolate and cream in the top of a double boiler over medium heat and stir until melted and smooth. Mix in the raspberry extract, if using. Transfer to a bowl and refrigerate for 20 minutes. Remove and stir, then refrigerate for a further 20 minutes. Repeat the process twice more and continue chilling for 4 hours or overnight.

Meanwhile, to make the pastry, sift the flour and cocoa together into a bowl. Place the butter and icing sugar in the bowl of an electric mixer and beat for 1–2 minutes or until light and creamy. Add the egg yolk and combine well. Add the flour mixture and beat until just combined. Shape into a disc, wrap in plastic wrap and refrigerate for 1–2 hours.

Preheat the oven to 180°C (350°F/Gas 4).

Roll the dough into 50 x 8 g (¼ oz) balls. Place each ball in a 3.5 cm (1¼ inch) fluted tartlet tin and press the pastry into the base and sides. Freeze for 10 minutes.

Place the pastry cases on baking trays and bake for 7–9 minutes or until golden and cooked. If the pastry puffs up, use a teaspoon to gently push it down. Cool in the tins for 8–10 minutes, then turn out onto wire racks to cool completely.

Transfer the chocolate mixture to the bowl of an electric mixer and beat on medium speed for 1–2 minutes or until soft peaks form. Transfer to a large piping bag fitted with a 5 mm (¼ inch) plain nozzle and pipe into the cases. Top with a raspberry.

MAKES ABOUT 50

400 g (14 oz) dark chocolate (65% cocoa solids), finely chopped

550 ml (19 fl oz) thickened cream

2 tablespoons natural raspberry extract (optional)

50 fresh raspberries

CHOCOLATE SHORTCRUST PASTRY

175 g (6 oz) plain (all-purpose) flour

25 g (1 oz) cocoa powder

125 g (4½ oz) unsalted butter, at room temperature

80 g (2¾ oz) icing (confectioners') sugar

1 egg yolk

warm apple pie bites

To make the dough, place the flour, sugar and butter in the bowl of a food processor and pulse until the mixture resembles breadcrumbs. Add the buttermilk and pulse until the dough comes together to form a ball. Turn out onto a floured surface, shape into a disc, wrap in plastic wrap and refrigerate for 2 hours.

Meanwhile, place the butter, apple, brown sugar, cinnamon and nutmeg in a frying pan over medium heat and cook for 5–6 minutes or until the apple has softened. Combine the orange juice and cornflour to make a paste, add to the apple mixture and cook for 1 minute or until thickened. Add the orange zest and cool to room temperature.

Roll out the dough on a floured surface to 3 mm (⅛ inch) and, using a 9 cm (3½ inch) round cutter, cut out circles. Re-roll the scraps and repeat. Place 2 teaspoons of apple mixture in the centre of each circle, fold in half and pinch the edges together firmly to seal. Refrigerate for 15–20 minutes.

Combine the caster sugar and extra cinnamon together in a shallow bowl and set aside.

Heat the oil in a deep-fryer or large, heavy-based frying pan to 175°C (340°F). Deep-fry the pies, 3–4 at a time, for 1–2 minutes on each side or until lightly golden. Drain on kitchen paper, then roll in the cinnamon sugar to coat. Serve immediately.

MAKES 15–16

20 g (¾ oz) unsalted butter

400 g (14 oz/about 3) granny smith apples, peeled, cored and diced

45 g (1⅔ oz/¼ cup lightly packed) soft brown sugar

½ teaspoon ground cinnamon, plus 2 teaspoons ground cinnamon extra, for coating

½ teaspoon ground nutmeg

2 tablespoons orange juice

2 teaspoons cornflour

2 teaspoons finely grated orange zest

220 g (7¾ oz/1 cup) caster (superfine) sugar

vegetable oil, for deep-frying

DOUGH

375 g (13 oz/2½ cups) plain (all-purpose) flour

2 teaspoons caster (superfine) sugar

150 g (5½ oz) cold unsalted butter, cut into 12 pieces

125 ml (4½ fl oz/½ cup) buttermilk

jelly appletinis

Place the juice, vodka, schnapps and sugar in a saucepan over medium heat and bring to a simmer, stirring until the sugar has dissolved. Remove from the heat.

Add the gelatine and stir until dissolved. Cool to room temperature, then divide among 12 x 100 ml (3½ fl oz) capacity jelly moulds. Refrigerate for 2–3 hours or until set.

Garnish with apple slices to serve.

MAKES 12

1 litre (35 fl oz/4 cups) apple juice

120 ml (4 fl oz) vodka

15 ml (½ fl oz) apple schnapps

200 g (7 oz) caster (superfine) sugar

1½ tablespoons powdered gelatine

apple slices, for garnish

black cherry
and kirsch jellies

Place the cherry juice, kirsch and sugar in a saucepan over medium heat and bring to a simmer, stirring until the sugar has dissolved. Remove from the heat.

Add the gelatine and stir until dissolved. Cool to room temperature, then divide among 12 x 100 ml (3½ fl oz) capacity jelly moulds. Divide the cherries among the moulds and refrigerate for 2–3 hours or until set.

To serve, turn out and garnish with the roses.

MAKES 12

1 litre (35 fl oz/4 cups) cherry juice

130 ml (4¼ fl oz) kirsch (cherry liqueur)

200 g (7 oz) caster (superfine) sugar

1½ tablespoons powdered gelatine

20 cherries, pitted and halved

dried miniature roses, for garnish

vanilla whoopie pies
with white chocolate chips

Preheat the oven to 175°C (340°F/Gas 3–4). Grease and flour 2 baking trays or 3 whoopie pie tins. Sift the flour, bicarbonate of soda and salt together into a large bowl. Place the sugar and butter in the bowl of an electric mixer and beat on medium speed for 1–2 minutes or until light and creamy. Add the vanilla seeds and egg and beat for a further minute. Reduce the speed and add the flour mixture, in 3 batches, alternating with the milk and beat until combined, scraping down the sides of the bowl as required.

Place 1½-tablespoon amounts of batter about 5 cm (2 inches) apart on the trays and bake for 8–10 minutes or until cooked through. Cool for 5 minutes on the trays, then transfer to wire racks to cool completely.

Meanwhile to make the buttercream, place the eggwhite and sugar in the top of a double boiler over medium heat and whisk for 3–4 minutes or until warm and the sugar has dissolved. Remove from the heat. Using electric beaters, beat the mixture on medium–high speed for 6–7 minutes or until glossy and stiff peaks form. Reduce the speed and add the butter, 1 cube at a time, beating well after each addition. Continue to beat for 2–3 minutes. Add the vanilla seeds and beat to combine.

Transfer to a piping bag fitted with a 1 cm (½ inch) plain nozzle and pipe 2 tablespoons of filling onto half of the cookies. Sandwich with the remaining cookies and roll the sides of the pies in the chocolate chips to coat.

MAKES 15

260 g (9¼ oz/1¾ cups) plain (all-purpose) flour

1 teaspoon bicarbonate of soda (baking soda)

pinch of salt

110 g (3¾ oz/½ cup) caster (superfine) sugar

95 g (3⅓ oz/½ cup lightly packed) soft brown sugar

125 g (4½ oz) unsalted butter

1 vanilla bean, split and seeds scraped

1 egg

250 ml (9 fl oz/1 cup) milk

170 g (6 oz/1 cup) mini white chocolate chips, for decoration

VANILLA BUTTERCREAM

3 eggwhites

145 g (5¼ oz/⅔ cup) caster (superfine) sugar

160 g (5⅔ oz) unsalted butter, cubed and at room temperature

1 vanilla bean, split and seeds scraped

mango lassi rum pops

Place all of the ingredients, except the sticks, in a large measuring jug and whisk to combine.

Pour into 18 x 60 ml (2 fl oz/¼ cup) capacity popsicle moulds. Cover with plastic wrap and insert a stick through the plastic into each pop. Freeze for 8–10 hours or until completely frozen.

MAKES 18

550 ml (19 fl oz) mango pulp

120 ml (4 fl oz) white rum

120 ml (4 fl oz) orange juice

250 g (9 oz/1 cup) honey-flavoured yoghurt

4 tablespoons honey

½ teaspoon ground cardamom

1 teaspoon orange blossom water

18 popsicle sticks

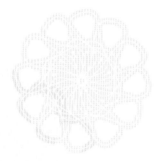

hazelnut macarons
with chocolate and frangelico

Line 2 baking trays with baking paper. Process the hazelnut and almond meal and icing sugar in a food processor until combined, then sift twice. Place the eggwhite in the bowl of an electric mixer and beat on medium speed until frothy, then increase the speed while gradually adding the caster sugar. Continue beating until stiff peaks form. Fold one-third into the hazelnut and almond mixture and combine well. Gently fold through the remaining eggwhite mixture; it should be glossy and thick, not thin and runny.

Transfer to a piping bag fitted with a 5 mm (¼ inch) plain nozzle and pipe 3 cm (1¼ inch) circles about 3 cm (1¼ inches) apart onto the trays. Leave at room temperature for 1–6 hours (depending on the humidity) or until a crust forms; the macarons should no longer be sticky to the touch.

Preheat the oven to 140°C (275°F/Gas 1). Bake the macarons for 15–18 minutes until they rise slightly. Immediately slide the macarons and paper off the trays onto wire racks to cool completely.

Meanwhile, to make the ganache, place all of the ingredients in the top of a double boiler over medium heat and stir until melted and smooth. Refrigerate for 20–25 minutes or until firm but pliable.

Transfer to a small piping bag fitted with a 1 cm (½ inch) plain nozzle and pipe about 1 teaspoon onto half of the macarons. Sandwich with the remaining macarons.

MAKES ABOUT 30

60 g (2¼ oz) hazelnut meal (ground hazelnut), plus extra, for sprinkling

60 g (2¼ oz) almond meal (ground almonds)

220 g (7¾ oz) icing (confectioners') sugar

110 g (3¾ oz) eggwhite

30 g (1 oz) caster (superfine) sugar

CHOCOLATE AND FRANGELICO GANACHE

110 g (3¾ oz) milk chocolate, chopped

3 tablespoons pouring (single) cream

50 ml (1¾ fl oz) frangelico

churros with
chilli-chocolate sauce

Heat the oil in a deep-fryer or wide, heavy-based frying pan to 175°C (340°F).

Place the butter, salt and 250 ml (9 fl oz/1 cup) water in a saucepan over medium heat and bring to the boil. Add the flour and stir vigorously with a wooden spoon until the dough comes together to form a ball. Remove from the heat and add the eggs, beating well to combine; the dough should be shiny and soft.

Transfer to a large piping bag fitted with a small star nozzle. Carefully hold the piping bag over the oil with one hand and a small knife in the other. Pipe the dough into the oil and use the knife to slice off 7 cm (2¾ inch) lengths. Deep-fry 10–12 churros at a time for 2–3 minutes or until golden and crisp. Drain on kitchen paper and keep warm. Repeat with the remaining dough.

To make the sauce, place the cream and chocolate in the top of a double boiler over medium heat and stir until melted and smooth. Add the vanilla extract, chilli powder and cinnamon and stir to combine. Remove from the heat and keep warm.

Combine the sugar and cinnamon in a shallow bowl and roll the churros in the mixture to coat. Serve with the sauce for dipping.

NOTE: Ancho chilli powder is available from gourmet food shops and delicatessens.

MAKES ABOUT 70

vegetable oil, for deep-frying

125 g (4½ oz) unsalted butter

¼ teaspoon salt

150 g (5½ oz/1 cup) plain (all-purpose) flour

2 eggs

145 g (5¼ oz/⅔ cup) caster (superfine) sugar

1½ teaspoons ground cinnamon

CHOCOLATE-CHILLI SAUCE

150 ml (5 fl oz) pouring (single) cream

150 g (5½ oz) dark chocolate chips (65% cocoa solids)

1 teaspoon natural vanilla extract

½ teaspoon ancho chilli powder (see note)

½ teaspoon ground cinnamon

glazed vanilla doughnuts
and doughnut holes

Line 2 baking trays with baking paper. Place 100 g (3½ oz) flour, sugar, yeast and salt in the bowl of an electric mixer and stir to combine. Place the milk and butter in a saucepan over medium heat and stir until melted. Add to the flour mixture and beat on medium speed to combine. Add the egg and beat for 2–3 minutes. Add the remaining flour and beat to combine well. Knead the dough on a floured surface for 3–4 minutes or until smooth. Place in a large oiled bowl, cover with plastic wrap and leave in a warm place for 1 hour or until doubled in size.

Roll out the dough on a floured surface to 5 mm (¼ inch) thick and, using a 5.5 cm (2¼ inch) round cutter, cut out circles. Use a 1 cm (½ inch) round cutter to cut out holes from the centre. Place the rings and holes on the trays. Re-roll the scraps and repeat. Cover and leave in a warm place for 35–40 minutes or until doubled in size.

Heat the oil in a deep-fryer or wide, heavy-based frying pan over medium heat to 175°C (340°F). Deep-fry the rings and holes, in batches, turning often, until golden. Drain on kitchen paper, then place on wire racks to cool completely.

To make the glaze, combine the icing sugar, milk and vanilla extract in a bowl. Spoon over the rings and holes.

To decorate, top with the sprinkles. Alternatively, for powdered doughnuts and holes, coat well in the sugar.

MAKES ABOUT 30

250 g (9 oz/1⅔ cups) plain (all-purpose) flour

3 tablespoons caster (superfine) sugar

1 x 7 g (¼ oz) sachet dried yeast

½ teaspoon salt

80 ml (2½ fl oz/⅓ cup) milk

25 g (1 oz) unsalted butter

1 egg

vegetable oil, for deep-frying

GLAZE

125 g (4½ oz/1 cup) icing (confectioners') sugar

1½–2 teaspoons milk

½ teaspoon natural vanilla extract

sprinkles or 90 g (3¼ oz/¾ cup) icing (confectioners' sugar), for decoration

pecan caramel tartlets

Preheat the oven to 180°C (350°F/Gas 4). Grease 24 x 30 ml (1 fl oz/⅛ cup) capacity mini-muffin holes.

To make the pastry, place the butter and cream cheese in the bowl of an electric mixer and beat on medium speed for 1–2 minutes or until combined. Add the flour, icing sugar and salt and beat to combine. Divide the pastry into 24 balls and place one in each muffin hole. Cover and refrigerate for 15–20 minutes.

Press the pastry into the base and sides of each hole. Cover and refrigerate until required.

Place the butter, corn syrup, honey and icing sugar in a saucepan over medium heat, bring to the boil and cook for 1 minute. Remove from the heat, add the pecans and vanilla extract and stir to combine. Spoon into the pastry cases and bake for 20–25 minutes or until set. Cool in the tins for 10 minutes, then remove and cool completely on wire racks.

NOTE: Dark corn syrup is available from speciality grocery shops.

MAKES 24

60 g (2¼ oz) unsalted butter

90 g (3¼ oz/¼ cup) dark corn syrup (see note)

1 tablespoon honey

65 g (2⅓ oz/½ cup) icing (confectioners') sugar

50 g (1¾ oz/½ cup) pecans, finely chopped

½ teaspoon natural vanilla extract

CREAM CHEESE PASTRY

125 g (4½ oz) butter, at room temperature

90 g (3¼ oz/⅓ cup) cup cream cheese, at room temperature

150 g (5½ oz/1 cup) plain (all-purpose) flour

30 g (1 oz/¼ cup) icing (confectioners') sugar

¼ teaspoon salt

mini coconut cakes

Preheat the oven to 180°C (350°F/Gas 4). Grease and flour a 12 x 125 ml (4½ fl oz/½ cup) capacity friand tin.

Place the butter and sugar in the bowl of an electric mixer and beat on medium speed for 1–2 minutes or until light and creamy. Add the egg and egg yolks, one at a time, beating well after each addition. Mix in the coconut extract and coconut milk. Add the flour, baking powder and bicarbonate of soda and beat for 1 minute. Mix in the coconut flakes.

Divide the mixture between the friand moulds and bake for 20–25 minutes or until golden and the cakes spring back lightly to the touch. Cool in the tin for 10 minutes, then turn out onto wire racks to cool completely.

To make the frosting, place the eggwhite, sugar, glucose and 2 tablespoons water in the top of a double boiler over medium heat and, using an electric beater, beat for 7 minutes or until stiff peaks form. Immediately frost the cakes and garnish with icing flowers or coconut flakes.

MAKES 12

125 g (4½ oz) butter, at room temperature

165 g (5¾ oz/¾ cup) caster (superfine) sugar

1 egg

2 egg yolks

2 teaspoons natural coconut extract

125 ml (4½ fl oz/½ cup) coconut milk

185 g (6½ oz/1¼ cup) plain (all-purpose) flour

¼ teaspoon baking powder

¼ teaspoon bicarbonate of soda (baking soda)

35 g (1¼ oz/⅔ cup) coconut flakes

COCONUT FROSTING

2 eggwhites

110 g (3¾ oz/½ cup) caster (superfine) sugar

3 tablespoons glucose syrup

icing flowers or 30 g (1 oz/½ cup) coconut flakes, toasted, for garnish

rocky road pops

To make the cake, preheat the oven to 180°C (350°F/Gas 4). Grease and line a 22 cm (8½ inch) round cake tin with baking paper. Sift the flour and cocoa together into a large bowl. Combine the sugar and 125 ml (4½ fl oz/½ cup) boiling water in the top of a double boiler over medium heat and stir until dissolved. Add the butter and chocolate and stir until melted and smooth. Cool slightly. Combine the egg and vanilla extract, add to the flour mixture and mix well. Add the chocolate mixture and mix well. Pour into the tin and bake for 30–35 minutes or until a skewer inserted into the centre comes out clean. Remove from the tin and cool completely on a wire rack. Finely crumble the cake into a large bowl.

Place the butter, icing sugar and cocoa in the bowl of an electric mixer and beat for 1–2 minutes or until light and creamy. Add the cream and mix well. Add to the cake crumbs and, using your hands, mix well; the mixture should stick together when squeezed.

Line 2 baking trays with baking paper. Roll the mixture into 30 g (1 oz) balls. Push 2 marshmallows into the centre of each and roll to enclose. Insert a stick into each, place on the trays and refrigerate for 30 minutes or until chilled and firm.

Carefully dip each pop in the chocolate, gently twirling off excess. Roll each in the walnuts to coat well. Stand in Styrofoam to dry. Serve immediately or store in an airtight container in the refrigerator for up to 3–4 days.

MAKES 30

80 g (2¾ oz) unsalted butter, at room temperature

125 g (4½ oz/1 cup) icing (confectioners') sugar

2 tablespoons cocoa powder

2 tablespoons pouring (single) cream

60 mini marshmallows

30 lollipop sticks

500 g (1 lb 2 oz) dark chocolate (65% cocoa solids), melted

125 g (4½ oz/1 cup) finely chopped walnuts

CHOCOLATE CAKE

110 g (3¾ oz/¾ cup) self-raising (self-rising) flour

40 g (1½ oz/⅓ cup) cocoa powder

200 g (7 oz) caster (superfine) sugar

80 g (2¾ oz) unsalted butter, at room temperature

125 g (4½ oz) dark chocolate (65% cocoa solids), finely chopped

2 eggs, lightly beaten

1 teaspoon natural vanilla extract

index

Published in 2011 by Hardie Grant Books

Hardie Grant Books (Australia)
85 High Street
Prahran, Victoria 3181
www.hardiegrant.com.au

Hardie Grant Books (UK)
Dudley House, North Suite
34–35 Southampton Street
London WC2E 7HF

National Library of Australia Cataloguing-in-Publication Data:

Bitesize: macarons, cake pops & cute things.
ISBN 9781742701165 (pbk.)
Cookies – Biscuits.
641.8654

Designer Trisha Garner
Editor Belinda So
Recipe writer Deborah Kaloper
Photographer Marina Oliphant
Stylist Caroline Velik
Home economists Andrea Geisler, Peta Gray and Lucinda Macdougall
Props provided by Bison Australia, ferm LIVING, Great Dane Furniture,
Mark Tuckey, Mud Australia, Nord Living and Safari Living
Colour reproduction by Splitting Image Colour Studio
Printed in China by 1010 Printing International Limited